my (w)alter ego

my (w)alter ego

poems by

walter w. hoelbling

© 2022 Walter W. Hoelbling. All rights reserved.
This material may not be reproduced in any form, published,
reprinted, recorded, performed, broadcast,
rewritten or redistributed without
the explicit permission of Walter W. Hoelbling.
All such actions are strictly prohibited by law.

Cover design by Shay Culligan
Inspired by a graphic of Gabriele Foissner and Beate Landen

ISBN: 978-1-63980-086-5

Kelsay Books
502 South 1040 East, A-119
American Fork, Utah 84003
Kelsaybooks.com

Dedicated to my parents and my grandmother
whose love, care, and unobtrusive role models
laid the foundations for the person
I am today.

Acknowledgments

Print Publications:
Journal for Transpersonal Studies 16:1: "summer in Verdun"
Love, Lust, Loss: "in this world," "then," "difficult words," "telephon call," "of course," "September 11–2001," "in this world"
Think Twice: "Leipzig 1990," "night sky," "short midlife crisis," "tending the heart," "full moon," "nature and me," "wind," "imagine," "it's time again"
Suffering in Literature/Leiden in der Literatur. Gedenkband für Sepp L. Tiefenthaler: "a very cold day"
English Studies 5: "wine country," "the abbot's tower of Montmajour"
JAWS 1: "autumn"
JAWS 2: "stoned"
JAWS 4, Vienna Views: "death at noon," "September 11, 2001"
JAWS 9: "going home"
JAWS 10: "he can do it"
De Consolatione Philologiae. Studies in Honor of Evelyn S. Firchow: "Milton Reconsidered," "hazards of the profession"
Almost All Aliens. Immigration, Race, and Colonialism in American History and Identity: "thanks-giving"
JAWS 19: "grey times"
JAWS 21: "dark moments"
A World Assembly of Poets: Contemporary Poems: "numbers game," "new solar system," "not for you," "poetry in the time of refugees"
Wild Daisies from the Side of the Road. A Collective Tribute to Maurice Kenny: "time travel," "when my time comes," "silence"

Online monitored publication sites:
gangan lit-mag, (www.gangan.at) "going home," "strange bird," "the loss of innocence," "liberation"
http://colloquium.upol.cz/coll02/02-pictures.htm#hoel
"September 11–II," "wine country," "imagine," "the abbot's tower of Montmajour," "short midlife crisis," "difficult words," "so easy," "distance," "then"
Tint 21: "spring has come"

Contents

natural wonders

autumn	15
winter colors on the island	17
summer evenings	18
bright day	19
night sky	20
rain's beauty	21
universe	22
no global warming	23
full moon	24
wine country	26
winter sky	28
nature & me	30
summernight storm	32
playing with words	33
wind	34
spring has come	36

a world of struggle

the shame of the world	41
our democracy	43
November 9, 2016	44
time travels	45
fake president	46
Helsinki	48
power games 101	49
poetry in times of refugees	50
why is it?!	51
smaller world	52
sweeter than honey	54
coming together	55

poetry in the time of terrorism	56
September 11 2001	57
Aleppo	60
Leipzig 1990	61
ach Vienna!!	64
Berlin 1990	65
summer in verdun	67
it's time again	68
cold world	70
dangerous harvest	71
virus	72
oh Corona	73
the mask	74
never in my life	75
patience is needed	76

from my balcony

humankind	79
so sorry	80
vegan thanksgiving	81
freely associating	82
beyond	83
we got it wrong	84
mirror, mirror…(found recently)	85
would we not	86
the abbot's tower of Montmajour	87
mothers all	89
let us remember	90
Halloween	91
beauty	92
difficult words	93
dark moments	94

cantata	95
find the words	96
the others	97

looking inward

strange bird	101
one night	102
not about you	103
the act	104
new solar system	105
when my time comes	106
birthday child	108
living	110
beyond sleep	112
shiny and bright	113
his hands	114
under my skin	116
Milton reconsidered	117
short midlife crisis	118
tending my heart	120
versifying	121
then	122
distance	124
temporary escape	125
why write anything?	126

natural wonders

Acknowledgments

autumn

quietly
over the past weeks
a gentle autumn sun
has painted colored leaves
upon the ground
and thinned
the bright abundance
of the wooded ranges

most of the harvest
is securely stored by now
or sold at morning markets
by weathered men and women
in country garbs

vintners are busy with their lots
fermenting grapes
and entertaining those
who see their visit
as pleasant pastime and escape
from daily urban chores

hunters and lumbermen
are waking up
to shoot and mark

schools by this time
have settled into the new year
teachers are happy still to share
the knowledge of our world
with students still inclined
to listen

businessmen
remembering their vacations
on the Bahamas or in Saint Tropez
step sprightly into offices
womanned by secretaries dreaming secretly
of beautiful Majorca summers
and of those never-ending nights
on the Algarve

I guess it is a human thing
to find a new beginning
and do best
when nature's breath goes easy
to collect the strength
for yet another fruitful year

or were it better
that we also took a rest?

winter colors on the island

rainstorms fiercely bulge the waves
toss honeysuckle and bougainvilleas
blow their blossoms high
towards the rainbow
that in sunny moments
sparkles over volcanic hills

summer evenings

the setting sun glows crimson over distant hills
people enjoy the balmy temperatures
sip their Mojitos and Manhattans
anticipating finger food and tapas
chatting with friends and neighbors

not everybody notices
the folding blossoms of the garden flowers
or the sweet evening songs of birds
the daring hedgehog venturing forth
    to look for food
the smell of honeysuckle gaining force
    under a rising moon

the beauty of our nature
often gets talked away in conversations
reduced to just a pleasant ambiance
that loosens our tongues

in our obsession to communicate
we tend to overlook the soft magnificence
the world presents to us in dusky evening hours

bright day

there are those days
so sunny and so bright
that you begin to think this is the time
for some achievement that excels
of which the people tell for many years
admiring stories of heroic deeds

the morning passes then the afternoon
the sun sets casually as usual
the moon is hiding behind clouds
and when night falls in earnest
shrouds the world in darkness
you recognize that though the day was bright
      it was the day not you
that people might remember

night sky

when I look up
   into a clear night sky
and feel
   the vastness of the universe
   touching me
it calls up
all the words
humankind has constructed
throughout millennia
so as to face the skies
   with dignity
and not go insane
   instantly
with this vague
   almost overpowering
sense of helpless awe
neither
the most sophisticated machines
   we send to the edges
   of our solar system
nor the most complex theories
can calm me
when I look up
into a clear night sky

rain's beauty

drops falling steadily
upon a misty world
far more than fifty shades of green
dazzle your senses
make you
    almost
hear
trees bushes flowers
drinking sustenance
    ecstatically
dancing in the rain

universe

when we think idle thoughts and diddle with our mind
we might as well just blandly look into the sky
and absent-mindedly pursue the flights of distant birds
against the matrix of blue firmaments
which seem less infinite than our imaginary universe

trying to look beyond that globe of blue
we venture into depths that really make us think
about the cosmos out in space
infinite stars and planets of unknown identity

we soon become aware
that our idle thoughts are dwarfed
by the immenseness of the space
through which not quite discovered forces
propel our planet with incredible speed
to destinies we do not know

perhaps in order to avoid acknowledgement
of this precarious reality
we fill our lives with more comforting things
fashions wars power games religion money
internet chats with other avatars et cetera

anything to distract us from the contemplation
of insights into how to live
   in such a transient indeterminacy
with a determined sense of goal and meaning

think about it

no global warming

when the tide is high
fish are splashing on main street
the ground water begins to taste
like the Atlantic ocean
soon Florida Margaritas will not need
salt on the rim of their cocktail glasses
their lemons will have enough

to protect its citizens
from the dire consequences of rising sea levels
the state government has acted
fast and furious
and has bann(on)ed terms like
"climate change" and "global warming"
from its official vocabulary

good job

[https://www.usatoday.com/story/weather/2015/03/09/florida-governor-climate-change-global-warming/24660287/]

full moon

one summer night
on the shores of Greece
I almost lost myself
coming home late
from a walk along the shore
   gingerly stepping
        between
sleeping bundles in the sand

the wind was soft
the sea warm
the moon full
   and hanging low

I shed my clothes
and swam
   southwestward
toward the moon

soon I left
the shore behind
swimming toward the moon
propelled by energy
   an ache
   primeval
   leg and arm

I swam
   like I never swam before

feeling I could go on
   forever
   very strong
swimming toward the moon

the moon now covered
all the horizon
and I swam right into
her golden light
in silken waters
that caressed my limbs

Dionysos calling

wine country

courting the sun
  after a cool June
  in my vintner's garden
close to the southern border
carefully sipping
  his latest selection
    a good year
    you can taste it

looking out from the hill
  across the river valley
  I listen to his children
  proudly telling how
only yesterday
  they filled 50 sandbags
just in case

the deafening roar
  of an interceptor jet
  splits the air
    just for seconds
    leaves my wine glass
    trembling

three helicopters
  slash their way south
  and come back later

over the winding road
  on the next hill
  the last tank of the column disappears

we can hear
  not far away
    over there
  sounds like explosions

we enjoy the sun

Helmut opens another one
  of his treasured bottles
  and tells me
  what he will do
  if They come across

he is a good hunter
and an excellent shot

I sip the clear wine
  watch how the sunlight
  lends its brilliance
  to the half-filled glass

I feel a little bit
  like Humphrey Bogart
  in the wrong movie

[Written at the beginning of the 10-day war in Slovenia in 1991]

winter sky

the lure
of the full moon's light
in a frosty December night
is almost irresistible

it beckons to you
its pale radiance
casts deep shadows
full of unknown possibilities
that grow by the moment
and struggle to turn into words
    trying to grasp the cosmos
    the mystery of life

 amazing how the mere reflection
    of the sun's brilliance
    can affect one so
it seems to ask you
to set a cool-hearted deed
make definite decisions
explore the blueprint of the universe
turn into a werewolf
dance with the dead

you look at the glimmering stars
    dotting the darkness
    left by the moon

delayed messengers
always too late

even with the speed of light
they only make us
    see the past
    mistake it for the present
    and build our future on it

the thoughts of a man staring at the sky
    in a frosty December night

deciding to love on

nature & me

wind is my friend
      blows my thoughts
      into lines
      like fish jumping for dragonflies
      on a hot summer afternoon

rain is my lover
      falls into me
      in steady gentle drops
      fills me till I am
      about to burst

sun is my brother
      warms my body
      with orioles of ancient light
      among dark shadows
      struggling to maintain
      their shapes

moon is my other
      casts a spell
      over the cricket's song
      the smell of honeysuckle
      the silhouettes
      of a silver world

wind goes on
      to blow on others
rain gathers its clouds
      and soaks someone else

sun goes down
        into darkness
moon turns so wan
        it hardly shows

I do not take it personally
nature is like that

summernight storm

poplar branches
embrace steel-blue clouds
so that they do not
tear off their tender arms
driven by thunder and lightening

the trees bend daringly
and you anticipate
the hissing sound
of splintering wood

it does not happen
the postures grow erect again
clouds disentangle themselves
and continue
their wild chase
for other arms

survived again

playing with words

I played with words
much like I fed the birds

   one morsel here
     another there

then suddenly became aware

they pulled together
   and made sense

have been a player ever since

wind

fierce
   fierce
blows the wind
   across this island
   off the coast of Africa
   where I live half of the year

here I am
sitting on the slope of a volcano
listening to the sound of things

street signs clatter to each other
empty beer cans roll noisily
   through midnight streets
doors keep slamming
   to make their presence known
plastic bags hiss airily
and fly away
   like they never thought
   they could

the ears
of the little dog that thinks
   I am his master
stand at odd angles
while he is grooming himself
   on my lap

        warm bodies
        in a blustery place

the patio chair
   scrapes its way
   across the tiles
   inch by windy inch

my wine slushes in the glass

I share fiesta music
   from half a mile away
   coming to me
   in gusty fragments
and almost feel the rush
   of low clouds chasing each other
   under a star-studded sky

here I am
on the slope of a volcano
listening to the sounds
of the world

spring has come

on the first day of spring
my mother died

she had always loved flowers
and had turned
our interior hallway
into a luscious greenhouse
  father was not always happy
  about the falling leaves

in her later years
when skiing was no longer hers
she hated winters
  their long nights
  their waning sun

she was always longing
    for spring
waiting for the day
the morning sun lit up
the kitchen counter again
in her parents' house
where she was born
and had grown old

the night before
I had called and told her
that here in Graz
the first flowers were already
dotting the gardens

she had smiled on the phone
    almost inaudibly
speaking had become difficult

maybe one of her last images
was that of colorful spring meadows

today at 7.10 a.m.
my mother died

spring has come

a world of struggle

the shame of the world

dead bodies floating
in our oceans
from the Asian Pacific
to the Mediterranean

crumpled corpses lying
on our beaches
thousands drowned unknown

overcrowded detention centers
      not unlike concentration camps
behind barbed wires
guarded by police and snarling dogs

nobody feels responsible

not those who started the wars
destroyed whole cities
made millions homeless
and into refugees

not those who take advantage
of the chaos for their own gain
abusing the names of their gods
or some ancient figureheads
to excuse their atrocities and greed

not those who live
in comfortable homes
and wish the desperate crowds
would just stay on the TV screen
and not come close

nor those who pretend
to be the guardians
of our great humanitarian heritage
but show no backbone
against nationalist fanatics

it is the shame of the world
to sit and talk and watch
and not do enough

   remember
   those who live by the sword
   shall die by the sword

and those who turn away
the needy and homeless
may also lose their homes
and have to rely
on the kindness of strangers

our democracy

at times we tend to think
our democracy is safely founded and secure
only eventually we recognize
the need to constantly defend its fundamental rights
work steadily against their stealthy abolition
watch carefully the words of politicians
    lest they betray what they pretend to say
think twice for whom we cast our votes
avoid contenders who too often bray
    that these were not their quotes
listen to those who have good arguments
    do not unleash too easy sentiments
and in the end cast our votes when called

in short
democracy turns out to be hard work

    and if we shirk this
    we soon pay the price

unfree societies have known
    dictatorship corruption vice
have often needed centuries
to remedy injuries done
to their four freedoms

and to recognize
democracy remains a living promise
a brilliant idea with many faces
always a work in progress

November 9, 2016

the day
when even the not so faithful
were tempted to pray
for the future of the nation

time travels

these days
looking around the globe
one might believe that we are traveling in time

just in the wrong direction

regression as progress
seems to be
the dominant notion of the day
creating wannabes in various disguises
    populist czars sultans nationalists dictators
    assorted self-appointed saviors
    of their peoples' wealth and health
trumpeting fences walls tough immigration laws
etc. etc.
to keep out all those aliens

    (who otherwise are welcome
    as our partners in the global trade
    that seems to dominate the world of greed)

so we can all be ourselves again

    whatever that might mean

claiming to solve the problems of tomorrow
    with fantasies of yesterday
is hopeless and quite dangerous

do you remember
what that glorified past
actually was?

fake president

talk shows and the yellow press
get excited in excess
over the shenanigans
that delight his faithful fans

rumors of these sex affairs
strong words for all macho players
    in the game of social thrones
texts with threatening undertones
    for minorities and women
    treating immigrants like demons

neither fans nor his opponents
seem to notice the components
of his white house strategy

    throw them bones
    fodder for the yellow press

and while they fight
clandestinely out of sight
works the Trumpian policy

money laundering blatant lies
scolding allies breaking ties
adoring foes praising those
    usurpers of democracies
    experts in atrocities
slowly yet persistently
    undermine civility
    with foul language
fill all courts with servile judges

court the aristocracies
    of oil sheikdoms in the East
praising communist dictators
who have helped him build his towers

step by step he's leading US
from the group of international powers
to an isolation desert
at the margins of the world
slogans we have rarely heard
over decades
    now re-nourished
twittered with presidential flourish
make America small again

    warning voices call in vain

no wonder the statue of liberty
is hiding her face in misery*

---

* This at the moment still is 'fake news'—but I would not be surprised if she did…!

Helsinki

two leaders once met in Helsinki
for talks that looked somewhat kinky
as it turns out
        still nobody knows
what they were talking about
and that indeed smells rather stinky

power games 101

1. Spread claims you are the only one who can stop corrupt politicians and their dependence on the rich (even though you yourself belong to the rich)
2. Spread lies and insults about anyone who might look like a serious opponent
3. Once you are in power, continue 1. & 2. and put your rich friends into influential positions in state offices and courts, give tax breaks to the rich and claim that everyone benefits from them. Declare any information that runs counter to your lies "fake news".
4. Invent threats to the security and well-being of the nation and then claim you are the one who can solve all the problems by strict measures, like building a 2,000 mile wall against those criminal immigrants that threaten your people—what the "fake news" reports as a few thousand refugees from neighboring countries who flee from misery and persecution and crime and hope to get asylum in your country of 350 million.
5. Cut your aid programs for the home countries of those refugees so that the situation there worsens even more and even more people will try to run for a better life, and you can rhetorically justify inhuman security measures at your borders.
6. On a different field, isolate your country internationally, be the elephant in the China Shop, break or end international agreements, destabilize whole regions, and then threaten to send the military—all of which, you tell your voters, makes your country great again.
7. Start trade wars with old global partners, accusing them of taking advantage of your country, and when your own economy suffers from such idiocies, calm your afflicted followers with federal subsidies that jolt the national deficit to singular heights.
8. Fire (or mob into retirement) any critical person in your government until all your officials speak with your voice.
9. Look around for a worthy cause to be the focus of your consolidated power.
10. Start a world war and lose it.

poetry in times of refugees

how do I write about the beauty of the world
when barefoot people pass before my window
in search of shelter

how do I share my pleasure of the birds' sweet song at dawn
when I see faces etched with panic
from the deafening blast of bombs

how to rejoice in love and friendship
when meeting people who could barely save their lives
after burying their loved ones

how can I write with passion of the kindness of the human heart
when I see thousands fleeing from the ruins of their homes
only to face police walls and barbed wire

true words are hard to find
as said a poet of an older war

   when it is a lie to speak
   a lie to keep silent

not easy

why is it?!

that over millenia
though major religions have advocated peace
their adherents have been slaughtering each other
    supposedly in the name of their assorted gods
more than any other known species

why is it
that in my maturity
    which people usually call old age
I'm getting so pissed off
with politicians who seem not to see
the obvious solution to a problem
but find elaborate fake excuses
just so they can get re-elected

why is it
that for Europe it's so difficult
to find a way for refugees to be accepted
with respect and dignity

why is it
that the USA apparently forgets it's been a country
living off its (il)legal (im)migrants for centuries
and now simply ignores the words
put onto their Statue of Liberty

why is it?!??

smaller world

you listen to what passes for the TV news
you read some
but not all
of social media views
you notice that
despite all internationalism
it's mostly old sensationalism
combined with more or less suggestive speculations about
how many people may have died in forest fires
to what imaginable depths the president aspires

whether the North Koreans have more rockets
    despite the wonderful achievements
    of the national superdealers
who of the leader's staff might be the next
    to lose her job or his credentials
etc. etc.

in short
the world has mostly shrunk
to domestic politics and power games
plus a few places on the globe where
U.S. soldiers still are dying
    in order to protect their country's interests
    in oil assorted mineral resources
    or allies of political expedience
or when a few thousand refugees from countries
    plagued by persecution or dictators
    are marching for weeks to claim asylum
        in the home of the brave and the free
        under the statue of liberty
    only to discover that they are seen
    as an invasion threatening

      that blessèd city upon a hill
visions have grown smaller
more petty voices dominate the talk

a nation made of immigrants
faced with the poor who flee from their oppressors
decides to close its borders to the immigrants' next wave
oblivious of the times when they themselves
still searching for a better life
found a new place where they felt safe
led by the statue's torch that shone its light
upon a poet's words of welcome:

"Give me your tired, your poor,
Your huddled masses yearning to breathe free,
The wretched refuse of your teeming shore.
Send these, the homeless, tempest-tost to me,
I lift my lamp beside the golden door!"

[The last stanza is a quote from the poem "The New Colossus" written by Emma Lazarus, written in 1883. For more information, check online at en.wikipedia.org/wiki/The New_Colossus]

sweeter than honey

to call hard science „fake news"
creates suspicion that this abuse
of hard facts about global warming
is but a shabby adorning
of the power of money
which tastes sweeter than honey
as lobbyists prove every morning

coming together

recently and repeatedly
after every massacre
by fanaticized or pathological idiots
politicians call upon their citizens
to come together
and pray for the murdered and their families

it is absolutely appropriate
to meet and right to do so

but it seems
that ever since 9/11
the nation only comes together
AFTER more of its members have been killed

 I very much wish
that the nation
   AND politicians
would come together
BEFORE the next massacre
and take action
to prevent such disasters
in the first place

poetry in the time of terrorism

when daily news
over weeks and months
report events that far exceed
most people's homespun nightmares

can we react as poets
and not be seen as cashing in on the sensation
like many media decide to do without regret?

it may be wise not to give in
to the temptation to create pornography of violence
but try to visualize the essence of catastrophe

a lonely high-heeled sandal on the roadside
one flip-flop much too small to fit adults
a tough man crying without shame

there are events for which
to find the proper words is very difficult

yet not even searching for them
makes them worse

September 11 2001

September has become
the cruelest month

reassembled
Hollywood disasters
at their worst
flipped into reality

as if
   we had needed that
as if
   we had not known
      that life is fragile
      and tall buildings
      can collapse
   taking thousands
   to sudden death

what is the point?

to prove
   that one can bring
   disaster
   to the undefended?

to demonstrate
   that minds bent
   on destruction
   can succeed
   if they plan long enough?

what a waste
   of lives and minds...
and more to follow
most likely

does wordless violence
solve anything?

the heartless deed
the glamorous sacrifice
that calls for more
   and more
       and more
neurotic spirals
of destruction retaliation
and revenge
instead of global peace
now looms spectral war
born from self-righteous pride
the need to strike out
   fast and hard
against whoever fits
intelligence-created data
transferred to screens
   meticulously marked
coolly oblivious of the people
   who work and procreate
      and live
   in those fluorescent blips

domesticated energy
serves the omnipotent
  two millionaires' sons
  turned publicl enemies
upon whose final global showdown
depends
the fate of yet more
  women
     men
        and children
to satisfy the need
for a just universe
where power flows
  undisturbed by laughter
  and the sounds
  of real people
    living
in a real world

Aleppo

one of the Orient's oldest
and most beautiful important cities
inhabited for thousands of years
by generations after generations
of craftsmen, merchants, artists, dynasties
famous architects of all styles and religions
the western end of the old silk road
home to over 2 million citizens
until not long ago

a few weeks of modern warfare
were enough to destroy
what hundreds of generations had built
for their lives as well as their sense of beauty

    rockets exploded churches, temples, and mosques
    artillery pulverized ancient palaces and new houses

    barrel bombs and poison gas
    killed the people

on tv we now see acres of urban wasteland
miles of rubble with no life
except for occasional tanks and soldiers
proclaiming victory over these ruins
in the name of a dictator whose regime
has become a puppet in global power games
no matter what the cost in lives or things

    to destroy is easy
    building things up is hard work

    with friends like these
    who needs enemies

Leipzig 1990

a city old in trades
in cultivation of the arts
based on industrious commerce
   of its citizens who boast
the world's oldest commercial fair

the city in which
Martin Luther and Melanchthon
led fierce disputes
with delegations of the Pope

where J. S. Bach found stimulus
and time to master
harmony and rhythm
close to perfection
(and that was shocked listening
to Leibniz's monadology)

the city of which
Goethe spoke with praise
that saw Napoleon defeated
on the nearby battlefield
(and built a monument of quite
imposing ugliness one hundred years
after the fact)

this city suffered hard
from two world wars
followed by over forty years
of dreams gone sour of a new society
until most recently
this city once again
became a catalyst of major change

yet those who held their meetings
at St. Niklas' church
and by their stubborn protest
helped to reunite
a country separated by walls for generations -
those you don't see
walking the streets of Leipzig now

what strikes the eye
(besides the crumbling blackened ruins
of former glory
and strip-mined land
just out of town)
is Wall Street's new frontier
the bustling peddlers of new easy wealth
as they appear on every street downtown
offering anything from oranges
to shoes and South Pacific cruises

ramshackle pre-fabs built on shabby parking lots
already stake the claims of big banks
business and insurance companies
that promise earnings, safety and security
to eager though bewildered customers

"Pecunia non olet" says the poster
  of the postal savings bank
  and shows a happy pig
  rooting in money

old stores, in order to survive
have started selling
new and shiny goods
to happy new consumers

only a few resist
and hesitate to walk a mile
for the mélange of
fast food, cigarettes and booze
offered at makeshift stands
that seem to symbolize
the great new freedom
of the new Wild East

[Written upon visiting Leipzig one year after the Iron Curtain came down."Pecunia non olet" (Latin proverb) = "Money doesn't smell!"]

ach Vienna!!

this time in Vienna
in my little nation's capital

a young Muslim still in search of himself
believes he has a mission
to kill as many infidels as possible
to avenge insults to Mohamed
and Allah by all those secular Westerners

armed with attack rifle handgun & machete
he shoots his way through the Vienna party mile
not knowing whom he attacks
killing four wounding twenty-three
among them four Muslims
driven by his duty to defend Allah

never questioning why the Almighty would ever need
to have his infinite greatness defended
by a confused youngster's shooting of innocents

[Apropos the attack in Vienna on November 2, 2020]

Berlin 1990

right in the eye
of history
I walk
among the crowds
that taste
the absence of confinement
   an unfamiliar space
between the bandstands
on the avenues
where people
test a freedom
   newly won
still strange
as yet in need
of daily reassurance

crossing and recrossing
   the big gate
   and the bridges
that for generations
connected nothing
marked divisions kept
   by guns and barbed wires
   and well-lit empty spaces
   between walls
   watched from towers

the new reunion
brings happy smiles for most
   quiet tears for some
new doubts for many
who are uncertain
   now

about their lives together
after decades
of separation

right in the eye
of history I walk

just now and then
a little bit afraid
that she might
rub her eye

just now

summer in verdun

the graveyards of Verdun
are full
with summer flowers

children are playing
hide and seek
among the crosses

their parents
   coke in hand
keep looking for the names
of their grand fathers
on the wooden beams
verifying the family album

swallows dive steeply
under darkening clouds
slowly approaching from the west

you try your best
to give them shapes
and faces
   them
who in grey noisy nights
fell out of life
   bright red leaves
   flushed prematurely
   by sudden frost

it's time again

when no mornings
follow nights
cities lie without their lights
little beasts root happily
children can live all their fears
   forest break
   mountains shake
then it's time again

rockets roar with deadly freight
sharp explosions rock the night
   soldiers shoot
   graveyards bloom
it is war

when scrawny skeletons
creep through the streets
parents weep
dead bodies radiate
   new death
and crumpled shapes
   spread more disease
then it's time again

the general orders strategic attacks
and watches how the metropolis cracks
   rivers stink
   battleships sink
it is war

when the bakers bake no more bread
when the butchers chop off their hands
when the doctors' only prescription is death
   corpses float in the village pond
   and supermarkets stay closed
        24 hours a day
then it's time again

maybe the ultimate time
for the warriors to storm from their heights
to the valleys to lance and destroy
   they also kill women
   all children are dead
   the moon is all red
   the stars are so wan

   we are counting the corpses
   as long as we can

it is war

[Written in January 2003, three months before the outbreak of the Iraq War.]

cold world

it seems we live in times
when helping hands extend only reluctantly
to those in dire need who had to leave
    the ruins of their devastated homes
    not waiting for more bombs to fall
to those who had to save their lives
    from the barbaric rule of self-styled prophets
and those whose simple love of education
    was met with inane terror and oppression

why is it that so many people
    are afraid of them and think
        these desperate refugees are perpetrators
            not the victims

why is it that the nations most responsible
    for chaos and destruction in these countries
        far from their own safe shores
    are the least willing to accommodate
    those they have driven from their homes

good Samaritans have become scarce
only a few today share their possessions
    with those who are in greater need

our humanity has been outsourced
to NGOs and sundry other institutions
to whom we donate so they feed
the hungry poor and the displaced

it makes one wonder whether shameless greed
has now indeed
    and without any saving grace
become the only goal of our race

dangerous harvest

those who are big of mouth
apparently believe that putting down the other
    calling them names & pepper them with slurs
might get them some advantage in the race
for the position that they crave

they better harken back
to the old wisdom of their mothers

those who sow dragon's teeth
will harvest dragons

virus

invisible
yet possibly deadly
it empties streets
makes us quarantine
cities regions nations
hits us unprepared
reminds us that pandemics
can also happen in our time

a few days ago I walked downtown
a strange quietness filled the air
made me react to noises and sounds
I had not even noticed
when streets were full with people and cars

    even the wail of distant ambulance sirens
    sounded louder and more ominous

I only saw occasional joggers
a few women airing their pet dogs
more bicycled food deliveries than usual

they hardly acknowledged my existence
glances did not meet
my friendly nods were rarely returned

solitary strangers we have become
keeping their safe distance

oh Corona

there once was a beer named Corona
preferred by those teens with 'persona'
they drank it with pride
but today they would hide
their delight has turned into a moaner

[Where are the times when Corona was just the name of a quite drinkable Mexican beer?]

the mask

it has become
the daily accessory
hated and loved alike
sign of bad times
and limited mobility

for some
   equanimously accepted
   as yet another fashion piece
for others a threatening symbol
   of prescribed orders from above
for many just a necessary nuisance
   they hope will go away in time

we certainly need to change
our reflexes upon the sight
of persons masked

 before Corona
    at least in our latitudes
masks were a sign of robbers and bandits

   now it's the good guys who wear them
   the bad guys who don't
   and … how can we be sure of that?

a real challenge to find out
just from the movement of the eyebrows
whether you face a friend
or not

never in my life

have I imagined
I would enter my bank masked
ask for money
and they give it to me
with a smile

patience is needed

in an age that brings instant gratification
by hitting a button or two
we are perplexed that good medication
cannot be found in a month or two

patience is waning so is dedication
after a month or two
no matter what the explanation
we start throwing a tantrum or two

in spite of our expectation
of a miracle or two
our desire for vaccination
      may have to wait
for a year or two

relearning to be patient in this situation
may give us a headache or two
when we surmise that salvation
      will not come
by hitting a button or two

from my balcony

humankind

the other day
I occupied a chair
at a sidewalk café
watching the vanity fair of the quotidian
float by in quickly changing apparitions

an endless flow of different ages nations fashions
skin colors miens postures & gaits
kept passing through my field of vision

it made me wonder why
some people get so furious
when they just hear about
   not even meet
   the 'others' different from themselves
that they start dropping bombs and shooting rockets

I think they rather should be curious
and eager to discover
how the immense variety of humankind
can help expand a locally grown mind

and recognize
that we are all of the same kind

so sorry

we look at TV screens that show
thousands of persecuted and bombed-out families
on the run for safety and sheer survival

so sorry

borders are shuttered now
the boat is full   no more come in
we have to think of ourselves

so sorry

we sincerely regret that you
are suffering from cold and rain and snow
in your rickety makeshift camps

so sorry

we are sure there's someone
to take care of all that mess
          it's just not us

so sorry

vegan thanksgiving

no dead birds in the oven
no innards in the stuffing
nor fatty drippings to be poured

the smell of roasted veggies
wafts through the wintry air
pumpkin and sweet potatoes
marshmallows green beans lentils
turnips & collard greens
hashed browns & black-eyed peas
quinoa sorghum cuscus hummus
carrots leak broccoli Romanesco
gumbo in southern regions
wild rice dishes in the north
tastily spiced with turmeric
cumin and baked paprika
Indian curry soy sauce chipotle
as well as with the usual suspects
of garlic salt and pepper
and whatever fits the taste of hosts

in short
a venerable feast to demonstrate
how nature feeds us a large cornucopia
of plants for our delight and sustenance

in short
no need to kill a bird

freely associating

love
dove
bird
hurt pain rain
washing laundry dryer shrunk
too hot   summer beach tanned skins
bikini girls   lifeguards bodybuilders
Schwarzenegger
robocop criminals politicians votes
lobbyists corporations   special interests
stock exchange oil price pipelines
pollution profits leaded water oily shores
banking wall street 99percent
wealth CEOs distribution education defloration
exploitation union struggle mc jobs
Walmart Amazon   tax evasion   offshore banking
islands caimans reptiles alligators walruses
snapping turtles manatees albatrosses
birds
dove
love

beyond

it is tempting to lose yourself
in the pleasure of worldly possessions
money cars yachts beautiful things

the Uncle Scrooge syndrome

as we know
even the pharaohs of ancient times
together with assorted kings and emperors
chiefs dukes presidents popes & cetera
could only take their toys
into their graves
and not beyond

we do not know for sure
   although we may believe
if immaterial possessions
have a better fate

yet even though we do not know
what our final moment brings

a thoughtful wrinkle on your brow
looks always better than
a bleak array of orphaned things

we got it wrong

it seems we got it wrong
in reverse
man made god in his own image

mirror, mirror…(found recently)

mirror, mirror on the wall...
what the hell happened?!

would we not

if we could
be someone completely different

at least for a while

child to adult woman to man
asylant to millionaire president to farmer
human to animal or tree

or vice versa

we can imagine all this
in our phantasies and virtual worlds
yet we are missing essentials

to BE a mouse a bear a shark
a president a film star a tree
is to feel think sense suffer
live in their alien worlds

maybe even understand

at least for a while

the abbot's tower of Montmajour

having just climbed
  through ages
up what seemed an endless flight
of narrow winding gothic spiral stairs
I step out
right into the wind's brute force
  instinctively
my arms grasp for a hold
fearful lest I blend suddenly
with the white horses
and the fields of the Camargue
far down below

wedged safely
in a nook of stone
a hefty tourist
leans out wide between the walls
toward the setting sun

her summer skirt is blown waist-high
revealing
unexpectedly delicate lace
above sturdy thighs

her body opens
to the strong soft touch
of the Mistral

a little later
she walks past me
clothes gathered
level gaze calm
self-assured

and leaves me wondering
whether the mighty abbot
on his solitary tower
and his exclusive brotherhood of men
had ever understood
the wind that blew
  and still blows
through two feet of stone
  like they were silk
and thrills a woman
to her bone

mothers all

for those whose mothers are no more
the annual business hype of what to give
    and where to take your mother
is but a sad remembrance of loss
stirring up memories of happier times
when she was still a pillar in your universe
loved and revered and sometimes feared
who taught you patiently or not
the basics of survival in your expanding world

she knew while you were as yet unaware
that all her loving preparations
would over time mean separation

when you struck out to shape your life
all by yourself and left her with her fears for you
her wishes and the hopes that what she tried
to give you was enough and right
your heart and mind were elsewhere far away
focused upon the future of your independent life

your years run fast and busy and suddenly one day
you stand before her coffin
and discover that it is too late
for all the questions never asked

what you have left are memories
and a vague sense of having missed the chance
to see - and maybe even understand a little -
the woman she has also been
throughout her life behind her loving face
of a dear mother's care and grace

let us remember

the myths of birth and rebirth
are as old as humankind

scratched onto cave walls
tablets of stone or clay
scrolls of papyrus or parchment
for hundreds of years on paper
and nowadays typed onto backlit screens
that are recycled faster
   than old hieroglyphs were understood

in our time
when refugees are tens of millions
on our globe
let us remember that these myths
have celebrated for millenia
   not battles war or death
but the survival of the human race
the joy we feel when new life has arrived
   often against all odds
the hope that emanates from goddesses
   or saints of yore
   who symbolize fertility
   have brought forth saviors and new tribes

these are what has propelled us to our current state

and we do well to not forget that our fate
does not depend on people slain
but on how we can save the joy of life
and celebrate all humankind again

Halloween

the night in which
the dead come alive for a while

only to be frightened
right back into their graves
by the horrible masked spectacles
of the living

beauty

over millennia the question
    what is beauty
has occupied the minds
of great philosophers

museums galleries and private homes
    as well as public monuments
display the sculptures paintings texts and movies
created by the artists of all cultures over time
with figures colors poems with(out) rhyme

looking at that variety
I do remember words of one much older
    "beauty is in the eye of the beholder"
Picasso speaks to one Velasquez to another
some prefer Shakespeare others e. e. cummings
in movies we find Billy Wilder or Fritz Lang
right next to Eastwood or Sarandon

which of them we enjoy with great abandon
depends on whether they can touch our heart and soul
move us to tears stir our thoughts
or simply leave us speechless

we have that soft spot for the beautiful
reminding us that there are things that go beyond ourselves

    they touch us gently
    like the morning songs of elves

till suddenly the brilliance of human art
reaches the very depths of our heart

difficult words

times are
when words seem
to have lost
their power
to be spoken

they stubbornly refuse
   to form
on the same lips
from which they flowed
only a heartbeat
ago

difficult words
they have become

   I love you

forgive me

   I love you

dark moments

predators of the soul
strike at the unexpected hour
having stalked their prey
for days and weeks and months

suddenly
the sun looks wan
and you know
they are there
waiting

when they attack
it's almost a relief
and yet
the struggle is
for life
or death

the beast of the jungle
is very strong

it is that other side
of your core
that rears its head
in dark moments

cantata

during a starless sleepness night
   when thoughts and feelings
   are confused but strong
I hear
Corelli's measured jubilating voices
praising God

and sense
a master's pride
   immodest
   in its musical perfection
   of transcendental adoration
reach out through centuries

the voice of human suffering
expectant of salvation
yet defiant
sounding victorious
even in its most humble moment
of timed defeat

the beauty of power
born from fragility

find the words

when we feel strong emotion
we often have no words
that seem to fit our commotion
we coo and chirp as do the birds
   or moo like cattle in their herds
and only gradually we find
the words connecting soul and mind
so we can speak our feeling
rather than reeling
   speechless
in some unspoken power's bind

the others

they are different
   just look at them
their skin color their clothing their speech
their customs   the way they move their bodies

we like them as tourists
they leave money in our country
and then go home again

   if they buy the house next to us
   that's different

it takes a conscious effort
to see them not as aliens
   but as our neighbors

unless we are aware
that all of us are aliens
in most countries of our globe

looking inward

strange bird

I am the night owl
flapping its wings
stealthily through your dreams
with a soft feathery touch
   you may remember
     you once imagined
like the figure at the end
   of the corridor
     whose face always remains
     in the shadow

I am the sower of images
   growing from the dark
touching your mind gently
tapping at forbidden doors
   closed to the brighter hours

I am the prowler of twilight thoughts
that lend shapes
   to your hopes
     and fears and desires
living their lives
   in between

I am the night owl
that shudders
   and folds its wings quietly
when the sun rises
   always too soon
patiently waiting again
until the day is done

one night

it happened once
upon a time

a place with a piano
much wine
& cozy talk
and when they left
tied in an amiable hug
heading for their separate quarters
each knew
the other shared
with someone else

she gently pulled him down
upon a Persian rug
lifted her skirts
quite irresistibly

they melted in bliss
knowing it would happen
only once
in their time

not about you

this poem
is not about you

even though
your spirit is in every word
your voice sounds strong
in the halls of my mind
telling me things
I am now sure
I want to know

this poem is
about me

trying to understand
you

the act

sometime it is
in the act of writing
that we create the sense
of what we want to say

as if the process of articulation
    when we are fishing for the proper words
is generating meaning
inventing itself in its own genesis

leaving the poet amazed

at times also the readers

new solar system

making love
suspends gravity
  and time
seconds expand
  into eternity
we are
  on top of the universe

floating
  in the fourth dimension
feeling
  the birth of a new solar system
    amidst convulsive explosions
  whose brilliance
    light years into the future
  may be observed
  by keen astronomers

we do not mind

our system
radiates and shines
in its time

nothing else matters

when my time comes

when my time comes
it comes
and I will gladly leave
to those who go on living
the task of sorting out
the mess I have accumulated
over years

let them discover
not only the stamp collection
the bank accounts
but also unknown niches
of their father's/friend's/husband's life
the words unspoken
scribbled on some paper
thoughts never shared
for lack of time or opportunity
the letters to a friend of yore
emails to many people
hints of potential
love affairs that maybe never happened
ideas to change the world
into a better place

here I am
  now with a 7 before my years
envisioning life after death

a sign of vanity
perhaps
or an expression of despair

I am not sure

it may just be
the fleeting thoughts
on a clear winter evening
when cold creeps slowly
but insistently
into your bones

reminding you

   of all that cold space
   in our universe
   how it grows larger by the second

making you wonder
if it has a plan
and if that plan
includes you
speculating
about your destiny

birthday child

a grandchild
   for her 9th birthday
very happy
   to be away from her older
   as well as her younger sister
  for a while
spent a long weekend
with her grands

   they picked her up
   schoolbag and bathing suit
   and guitar & everything else

she had already mentioned
   that French Toast for breakfast
would be REALLY nice
that's what she got
together with chocolate milk
   1 minute in the microwave
   according to her wish
patiently reading her book
while the oldies got their act together
   in their slow morning routine

they all went birthday shopping
   & out for lunch
she read her book again while the oldies
   were snoring their nap
& then they all had great fun
   swimming and horsing around in the pool

  watching some TV
   & improving her ping-pong game
happy & tired

after dinner some goodnight reading
doughnuts and hot chocolate for breakfast
next morning
   and then
     with grandma's help
printing out a card for Mom on Mother's day
AND baking real brownies as a gift....

a happy & proud 9-year old
   was delivered to her parents
& presented her mother with the card
   & the brownies & the new dress
   & the homework all done
somehow
the guitar practice had gotten lost

yet she was the envy of her siblings
for the day

living

I sit
  all by myself
  again
and look out
  down upon the streets
cigarette in hand
a glass of wine upon the table
love's sweet exhaustion lingering in my bones
  and smell upon my skin
feeling so young and yet somehow so old

a late night bus drones by
and takes strange people
  to desired stops
in a city
where I know only few
that could say
 yes
 it's him

a woman with unsteady midnight gait
secretly walks her dog
into the public park
  both little more than blurs
  of bluish white and brown
  in the half-shadow
  of forbidden bushes

a couple leans entwined
  forever in a parting kiss
  upon the doorstep
unmindful of the plane
  that comes in low and loud
  before the landing

why is it that these moments
   seem eternal and yet
I sense the rush of time go fast
   and pass me by
   and her
   who sleeps next door
and leave us lost among our memories
of what was lovely
   and so beautiful
   before

beyond sleep

they told me
my father died quietly
in his sleep
at 3 a.m.

with his pain-ridden last years
I think he was not unhappy
to go farther for once
return to the cosmos he came from
wake up painless
    at peace
floating in the universe
he had admired from mountain peaks
all of his life

shiny and bright

my friends said last night
I should write something light
something shiny and bright
to the readers' delight

no fights and no terror
no soldiers no war
no suicide bombers
no refugees galore

after all it's the season
when together we sing
of the love that we bring
to each other
    within reason

so I am doing my best
not to make a clean breast
    of the worries that plague me
cuddle deep in my nest
only welcome the guests
who bring me good news
and carefully wipe
all the dirt from their shoes
ere they enter my house

so to rouse our good feelings
we all listen to the chimes
of the church bells so pealing

and to a poem that rhymes

his hands

when the telephone rang
at six in the morning
four days before Christmas Eve
   I knew
things were not right

they told me
   my father had died
   at three in the morning
   and would I please come by
   arrange for the burial
   and collect his belongings
at the senior citizens home
where he had spent
the last four years
of his life

they had rested him nicely
he looked at peace
I kissed him on his forehead
   like I always had
   at the end of my visits
and cast a last long look at his figure
   before the body would be taken away

   and suddenly I noticed
     how big his hands were
   they'd never seemed so prominent before

as if in death they sent me a reminder
of how much he had loved his hands
   for work   for play for sports
   for fight and for survival
   to point and to gesticulate

they held me as a baby and
     some times
   slapped me as a child
  they repaired toys   split wood
  built sheds   drove cars and motor bikes
  were patient and precise
  caressed and soothed and loved

they were his life
they held his world

my father's hands

under my skin

my eyes
  see yours
when they awake
to face the world

your lips
return my smile
in dreamy moments

your face
looks into mine
from my reflections
in the polished glass

my voice responds
   to yours
in endless dialogue
through time and space

your body's loving warmth
has taken home
deep down within

I have got you
under my skin

Milton reconsidered

when I consider how my days are spent
with work that leads to work with little time for meditation
except for a few moments now and then
on trains or planes or in the car
at times I feel our Western civilization
may not have taken us so very far

not that I am ungrateful for electric light
it eases one of our deepest fears
of nights that cast a dazzling darkness on creation
until another sun returns it to our appreciation.

yet I do wonder if our brilliant sight
derived from deftly harnessed natural powers
makes us indeed see more of that strange world of ours
than saw an old man's dimming vision under candlelight

[Inspired by John Milton's "On His Blindness."]

short midlife crisis

a certain morning stiffness
in your joints

you find your face
in the bathroom mirror
and wish you hadn't

the puzzled wisdom
   of middle age
wavers from your eyes
deepening wrinkles
  of many laughs
  many frowns

  how many more?

nevermore ?!

the room becomes aflutter
with Poesque ravens
the presence of absences
fills the void
your life is on the brink
of deconstructing itself
to the periphery of the universe
a discourse of silence
forever becoming ... becoming ...
what?

nevermind!

so

you close your eyes
   hard
for a minute or two

when you look again
you meet the stare
of a not-so-bad-looking
man in his best years

   graying sideburns
   receding hairline
   20 pounds too many
      BUT
   a firm decision
   to work them off

   still a bit sleepy
   yet determined
   to shave
      get dressed
      have breakfast

and teach
that wonderful seminar
on 19th century U. S. poetry
to eager graduate students

tending my heart

now and again
I tend my heart
leave facts and figures behind
and enter the realm of feeling
where
   as in a primal ocean
float beings about to become
   not easy to classify
   almost before words

somewhat like a school
   of amorphous translucent jellyfish
   good vibes float towards
   a loved one
predatory shapes speed by
   to attack unfriendlies
luminous orange-blue flowers
shine in the wake
   of good food and company
a bright red coral reef
   hovers like a loving kiss
tumultuous slashing of the waves
   feels strong and overwhelming
   in blue-lit foamy white

I float back to the surface
   and
looking at the sky
   whose blue is as deceptive
   as that of the waters
I wait for my heart
to tell me
which one
to trust

versifying

thinking of things to put to verse
   in times that often are adverse
   to topics that involve the universe
   and other serious matter
is difficult

world politics is quite atrocious
the culture scene no less ferocious
and so if you are somewhat cautious
in your choice of themes
few are left

you might start out with poised pen
for something serious & pertinent - but then
you have a quite inspiring moment when
you realize what truly is important
in our lives

just find the words
others can understand

then

thinking of times
when walking for a mile
took you into a different world
climbing a hill
   through clinging underbrush
filled you with apprehension
of what might be awaiting you
beyond the crest

then
to slowly open up
the pages of a book
was always more
than just a ritual of escape

the not so casual touch
   of a girl's hard breast
   a boy's lean hand
upon your shoulder
sent shudders down your spine
of inarticulate hot expectations
and brought wild images to you
at night
in lusting isolation

to keep this core
   the sense of awe
   of wonder and excitement
alive in you against the waves of many years
is not an easy feat
   yet worth the while

it makes you see
   when many just walk by
life's gracious beauty in small moments

distance

the world is slowing down
a mist of milky gossamer moves in
      between
my will and things to do
the clear shapes of objects
are growing soft and dull
the moment's urgency
yields to my ponderings
  of possible decisions
abstract rigidity arrests the words
things stay forever as they are

is it a sense of death
that delicately touches at my neck
and steals from me the comfort
of continuous change?

life seems to walk away
in long and measured stride
the kitchen clock has never run so fast

      it measures time
      from here up to the stars

it counts
    and blows
the moments of my delicate eternity
    one by one
into the past

temporary escape

on an enchanted summer evening
the world feels wonderful and meek

why do I still crave more
   than I can feel and seek

why do I need to go beyond the pastoral
   trust the smooth surface
   of this world
   only for blissful moments

feel almost something like relief
when daily imperfections
crowd me again and throw me hard
into the maelstrom of those obligations
that have accumulated over years
tell me I have matured and know
what all life really is about

but also loudly shout
   I do not know
the meaning of my life

yet I envision in the hour of my death
my last breath will flow easy
   with no strife

remembering the summer evening
I have spent my life to seek
so wonderful …
   and mild …
      and meek …

why write anything?

sometimes I wonder why I bother
to force myself to tell an other
what are my feelings and opinions

why do I struggle to attempt to phrase
words that inhabitants of faraway dominions
might also understand and not erase
an alien text for lack of recognition
of what it tries to say

is it just egomaniacal vanity
born of conviction that my words
are so important that only nerds
would not appreciate the wisdom
inherent in my thoughts

or is it logorrhea the pathological obsession
to spew forth words without control
and flood the world and every living soul
with streams of endless syntax without meaning

I guess I write in order to communicate and share
exchange ideas across all boundaries
learning the thoughts of many different people
and in the process become even more aware
how much we share and how much not

carrying away once more the recognition
that division has for ages been
    and still remains until this day
the favorite tool of greedy politicians
against which poets firmly must hold sway

About the Author

Walter W. Hoelbling, born in1947 in a little district town 100 km southeast of Vienna, is a retired professor of U.S. Literature and Culture at the American Studies Department of Karl-Franzens-University in Graz, Austria. Among his authored and co-edited publications are *The European Emigrant Experience in the U. S. A, Nature's Nation' Revisited: American Concepts of Nature from Wonder to Ecological Crisis, What Is American? New Identities in U. S. Culture, U. S. Icons and Iconicity,* and *Theories and Texts. For Students By Students,* as well as a good number of articles on American Studies in Europe, U. S. war fiction and film, Indian captivity narratives, US postmodern and postcolonial fiction, and the affinities of U.S. literature and film to public political rhetoric.
As Visiting Scholar he did research at Rutgers University, NJ; Columbia University, NY; SUNY Albany, NY; Stanford University, and the Univ. of Michigan, Ann Arbor; as Visiting Professor he taught at the University of Minnesota Dept. of English in Minneapolis for two quarters. He started writing poetry in English in the late 1970s and has published two volumes of poetry in English—*Love Lust Loss* (2003) and *Think Twice* (2006), together with Gabriele Poetscher, former colleague from the Graz University English Department. With her he also co-edited *Myself and Others,* #37 of *Gangan Lit-Mag*.

More recently he published a volume of German language poems (*Gemischter Satz. Gedichte,* 2018; 2020), and he also contributes to poetry journals and collections in print and online.

www.ingramcontent.com/pod-product-compliance
Lightning Source LLC
Chambersburg PA
CBHW032232080426
42735CB00008B/816